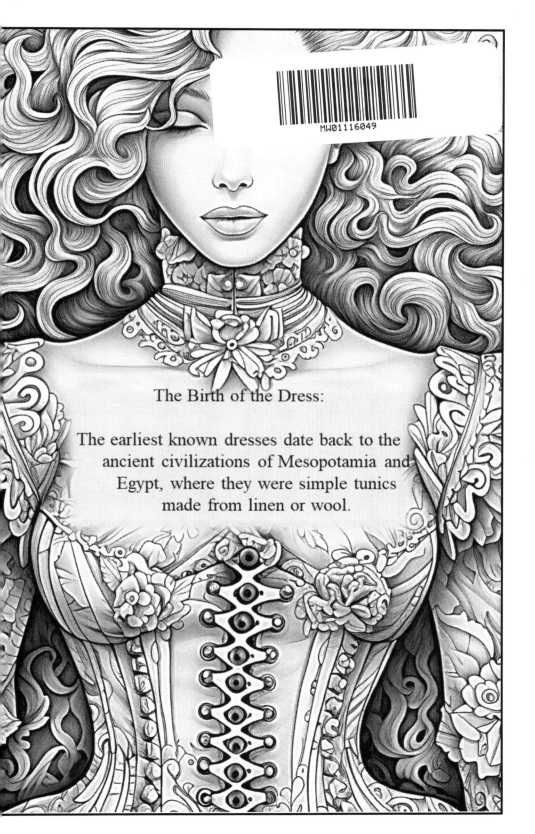

The Birth of the Dress:

The earliest known dresses date back to the ancient civilizations of Mesopotamia and Egypt, where they were simple tunics made from linen or wool.

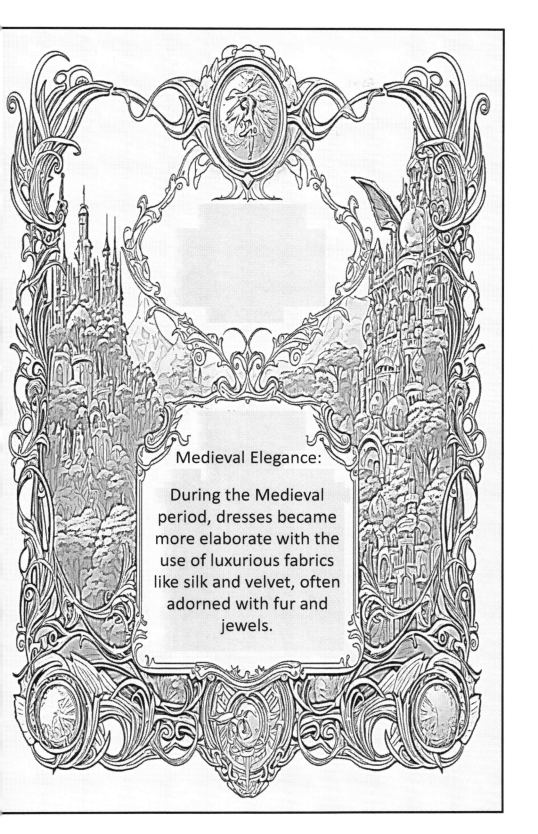

Medieval Elegance:

During the Medieval period, dresses became more elaborate with the use of luxurious fabrics like silk and velvet, often adorned with fur and jewels.

Renaissance
Revolution:

The Renaissance era saw
dresses with intricate
designs, including
corseted bodices and full
skirts supported by
farthingales.

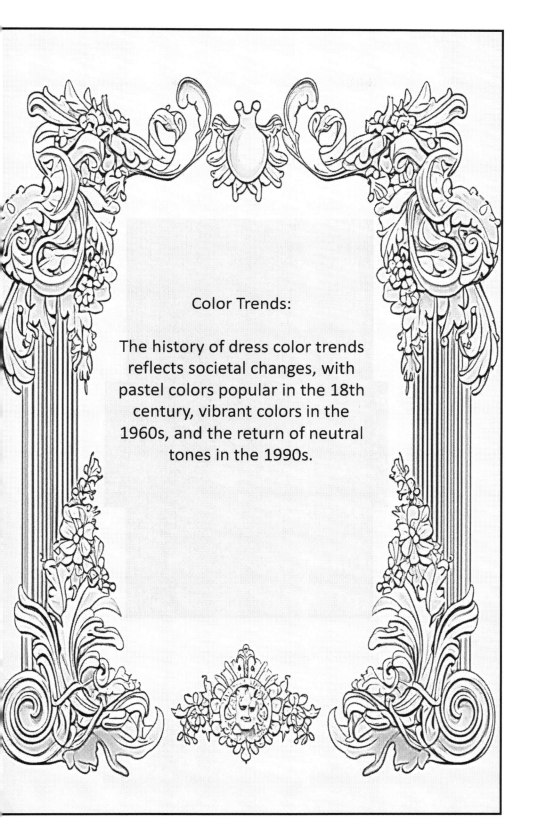

Color Trends:

The history of dress color trends reflects societal changes, with pastel colors popular in the 18th century, vibrant colors in the 1960s, and the return of neutral tones in the 1990s.

The Baroque and
Rococo Influence:

These periods
introduced more
opulence with heavy
brocades, lace, and
embroidered fabrics,
showcasing the wealth
and status of the
wearer.

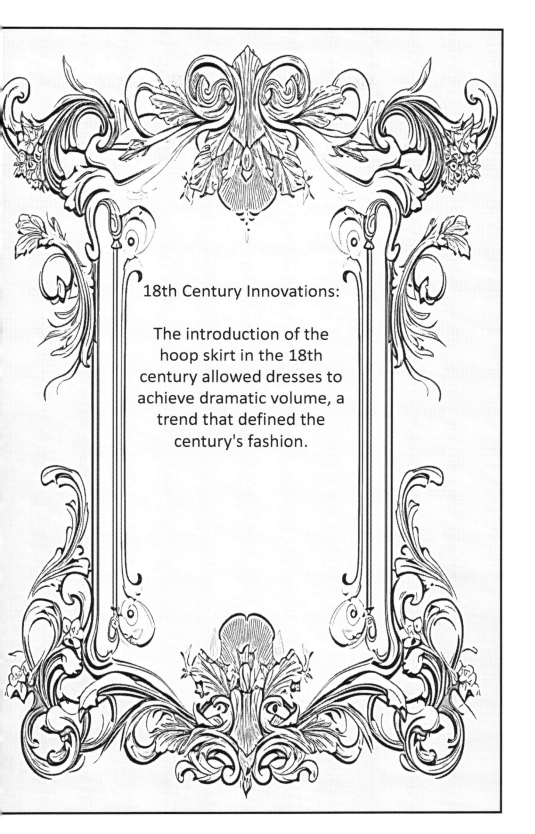

18th Century Innovations:

The introduction of the hoop skirt in the 18th century allowed dresses to achieve dramatic volume, a trend that defined the century's fashion.

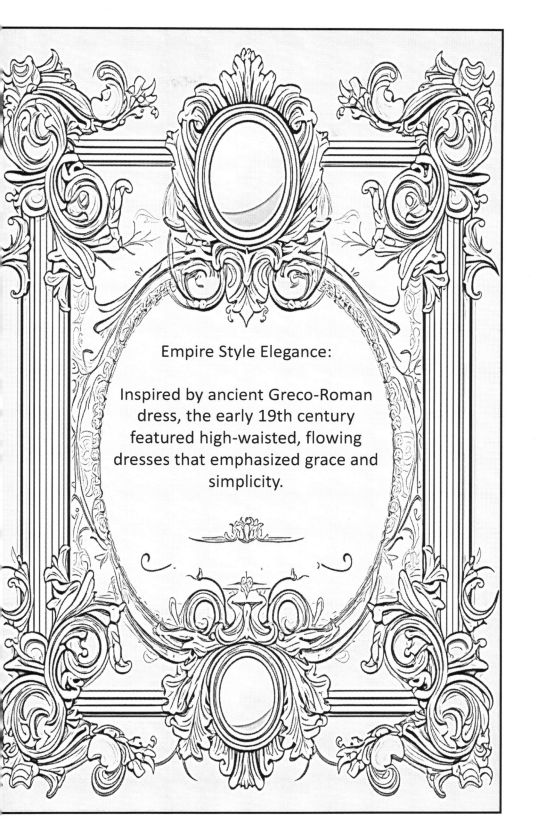

Empire Style Elegance:

Inspired by ancient Greco-Roman dress, the early 19th century featured high-waisted, flowing dresses that emphasized grace and simplicity.

Victorian
Complexity:

The Victorian era is
known for its
intricate dress
designs, including
crinolines, bustles,
and elaborate
trimmings that
highlighted a
woman's waist.

The Birth of Haute Couture: Charles Frederick Worth, considered the father of haute couture, revolutionized fashion in the 19th century by creating custom-made, elaborate dresses for the elite.

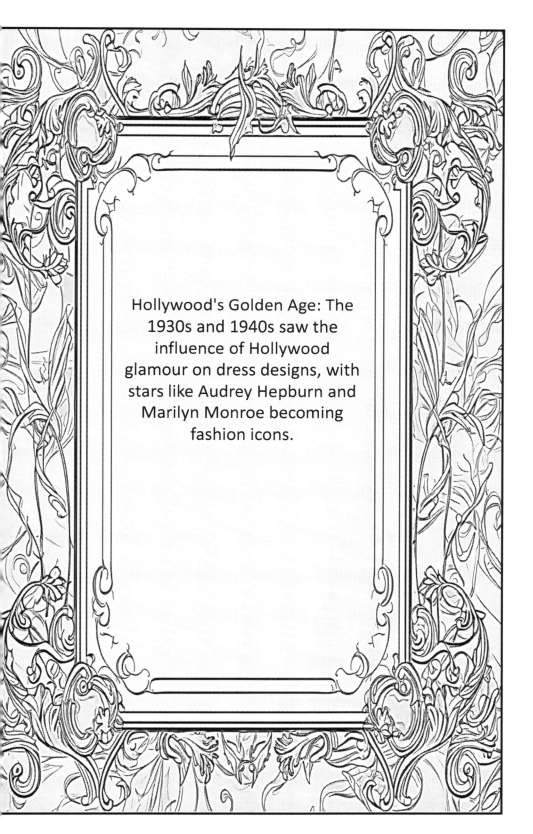

Hollywood's Golden Age: The 1930s and 1940s saw the influence of Hollywood glamour on dress designs, with stars like Audrey Hepburn and Marilyn Monroe becoming fashion icons.

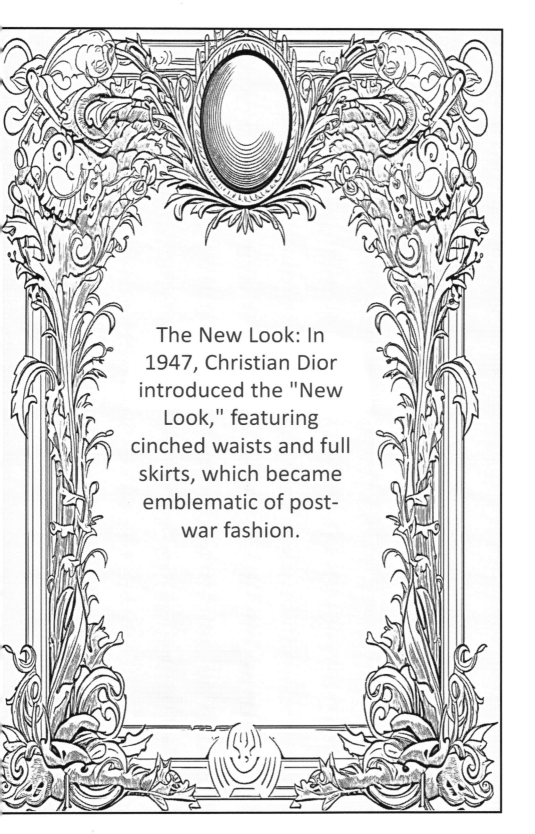

The New Look: In 1947, Christian Dior introduced the "New Look," featuring cinched waists and full skirts, which became emblematic of post-war fashion.

Mod Fashion and Mini Dresses: The 1960s introduced mod fashion, with the mini dress becoming a symbol of youthful rebellion and freedom.

Punk Rock Rebellion: The 1970s punk movement brought a DIY aesthetic to dresses, incorporating elements like safety pins, chains, and leather.

Flapper Freedom: The 1920s introduced the flapper dress, characterized by its loose fit and shorter hemlines, reflecting women's increasing independence.

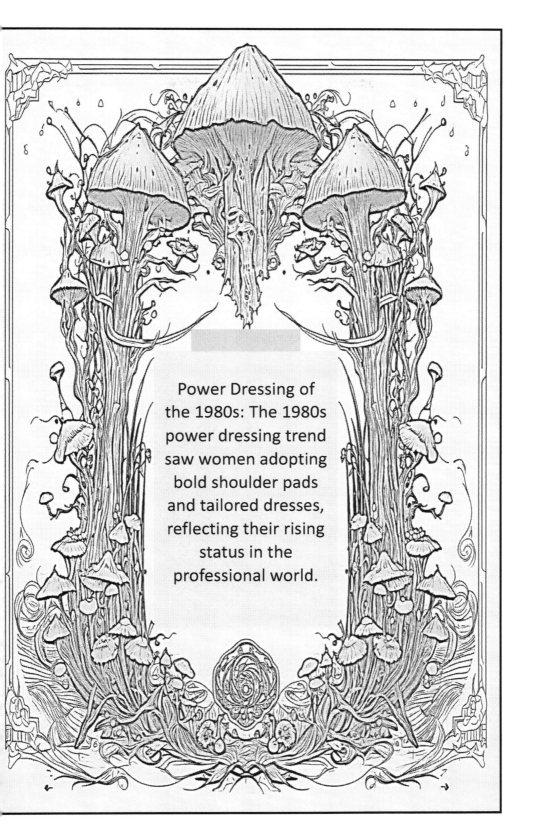

Power Dressing of the 1980s: The 1980s power dressing trend saw women adopting bold shoulder pads and tailored dresses, reflecting their rising status in the professional world.

Minimalism of the 1990s: The 1990s embraced minimalism, with simple, sleek dresses that moved away from the excesses of the previous decade.

The Rise of Sustainable Fashion: The 21st century has seen a growing focus on sustainable and ethical dressmaking practices, reflecting a shift towards environmental consciousness in fashion.

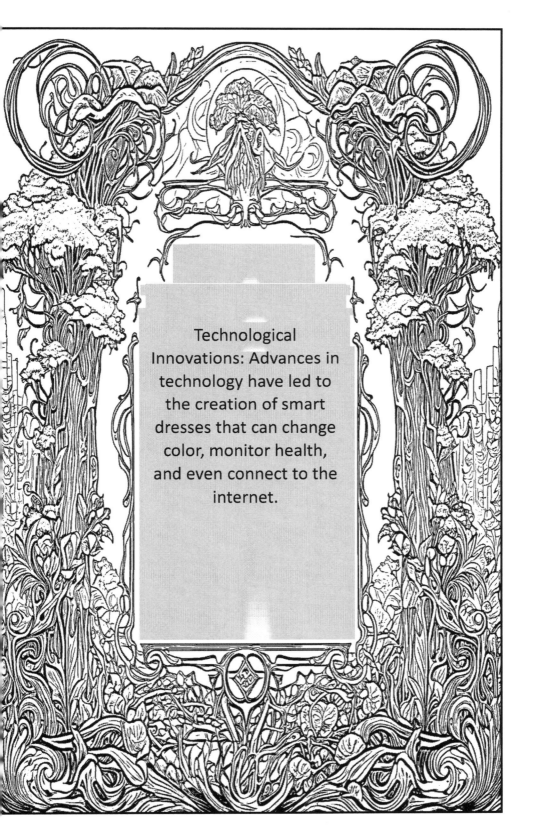

Technological Innovations: Advances in technology have led to the creation of smart dresses that can change color, monitor health, and even connect to the internet.

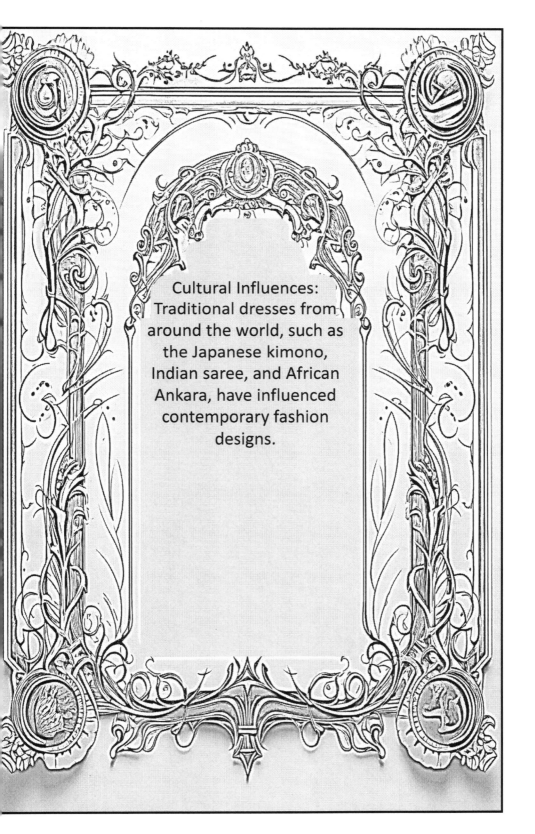

Cultural Influences: Traditional dresses from around the world, such as the Japanese kimono, Indian saree, and African Ankara, have influenced contemporary fashion designs.

Iconic Dresses in History: Some dresses have become iconic, such as Princess Diana's wedding dress and the little black dress popularized by Coco Chanel.

Fashion Museums: Institutions like the Metropolitan Museum of Art's Costume Institute in New York and the Musée de la Mode in Paris preserve and exhibit the history of dressmaking.

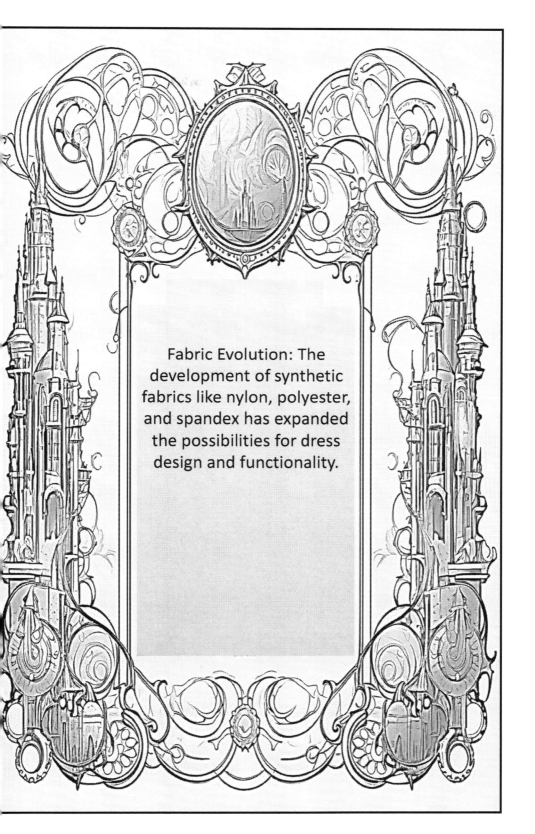

Fabric Evolution: The development of synthetic fabrics like nylon, polyester, and spandex has expanded the possibilities for dress design and functionality.

Royal Influence: Royalty has historically influenced dress trends, with Queen Victoria popularizing white wedding dresses in the 19th century.

Designer Impact:
Designers like Yves Saint
Laurent, who introduced
the tuxedo dress for
women, have played
pivotal roles in
challenging and reshaping
traditional dress norms.

The Wrap Dress: Introduced by Diane von Fürstenberg in the 1970s, the wrap dress is celebrated for its versatility and flattering design for all body types.

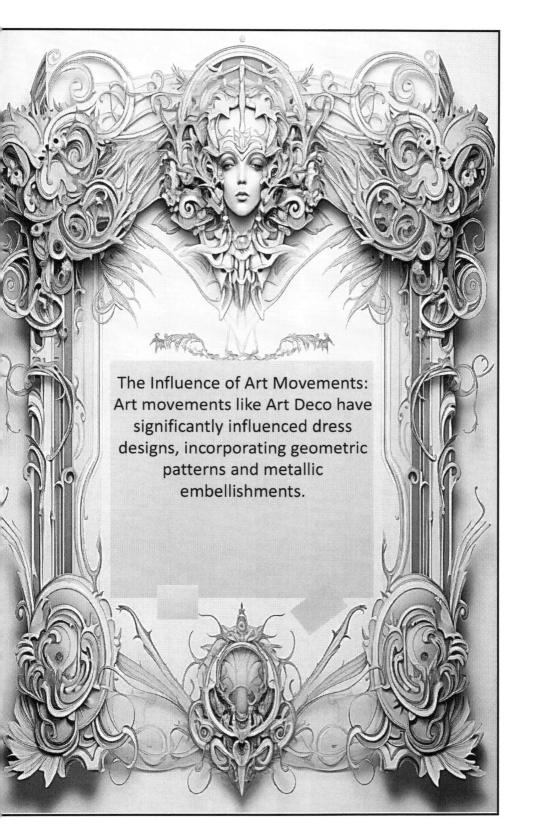

The Influence of Art Movements:
Art movements like Art Deco have
significantly influenced dress
designs, incorporating geometric
patterns and metallic
embellishments.

Fashion Weeks: Paris, Milan, London, and New York Fashion Weeks are pivotal in shaping global dress trends and showcasing the latest in dress design.

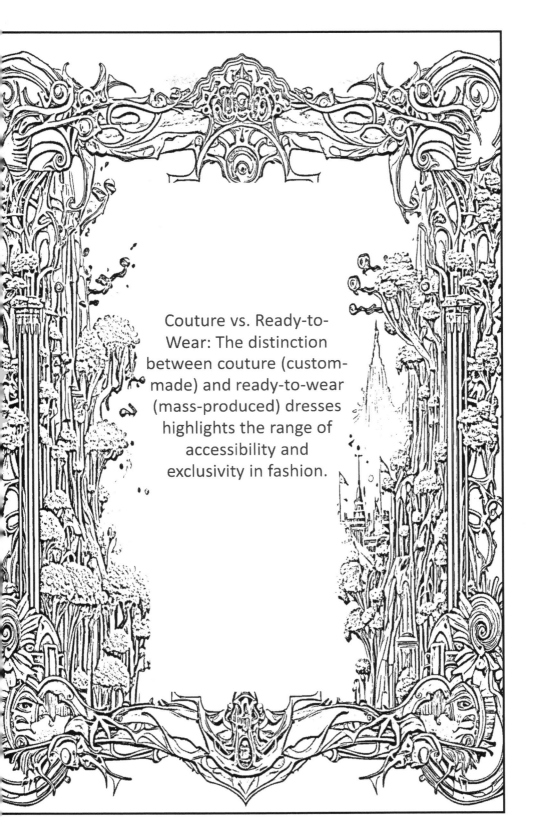

Couture vs. Ready-to-Wear: The distinction between couture (custom-made) and ready-to-wear (mass-produced) dresses highlights the range of accessibility and exclusivity in fashion.

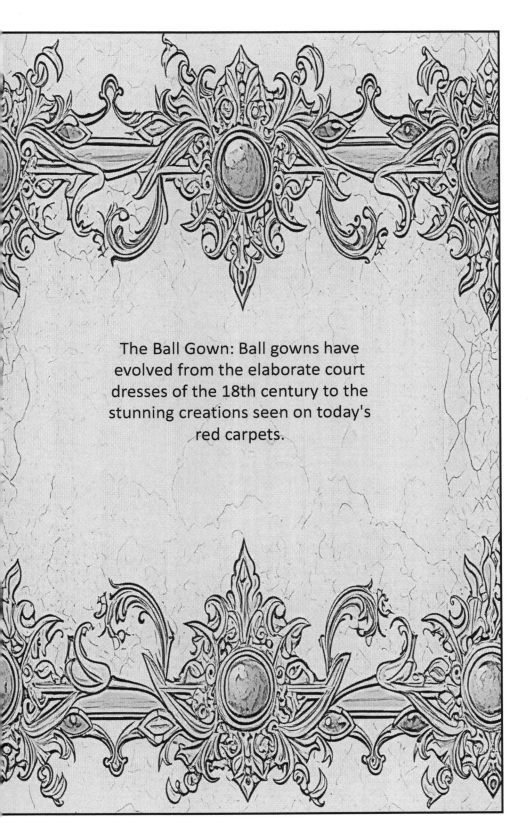

The Ball Gown: Ball gowns have evolved from the elaborate court dresses of the 18th century to the stunning creations seen on today's red carpets.

Dress Codes and Social Norms: Dress codes, from the strict sumptuary laws of the past to modern-day black-tie events, have long influenced dress designs and fashion choices.

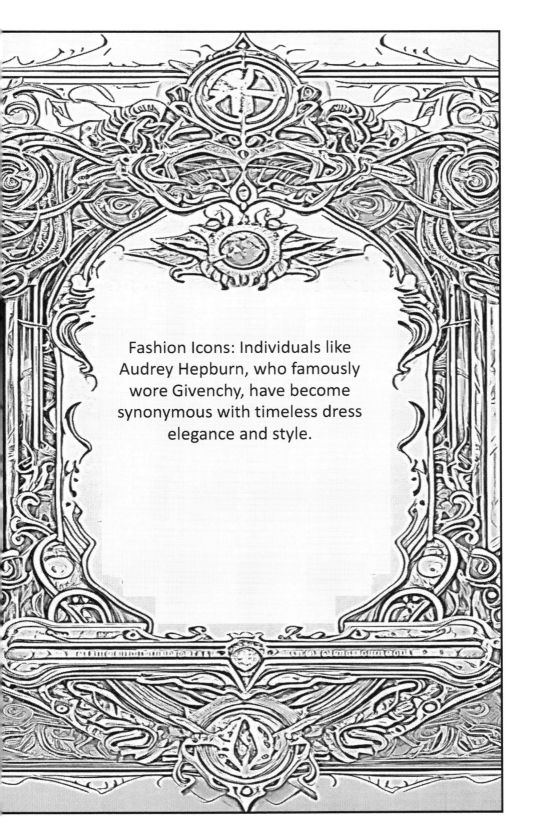

Fashion Icons: Individuals like Audrey Hepburn, who famously wore Givenchy, have become synonymous with timeless dress elegance and style.

Innovative Materials: The use of innovative materials, such as LED fabrics and 3D printed elements, is pushing the boundaries of traditional dressmaking.

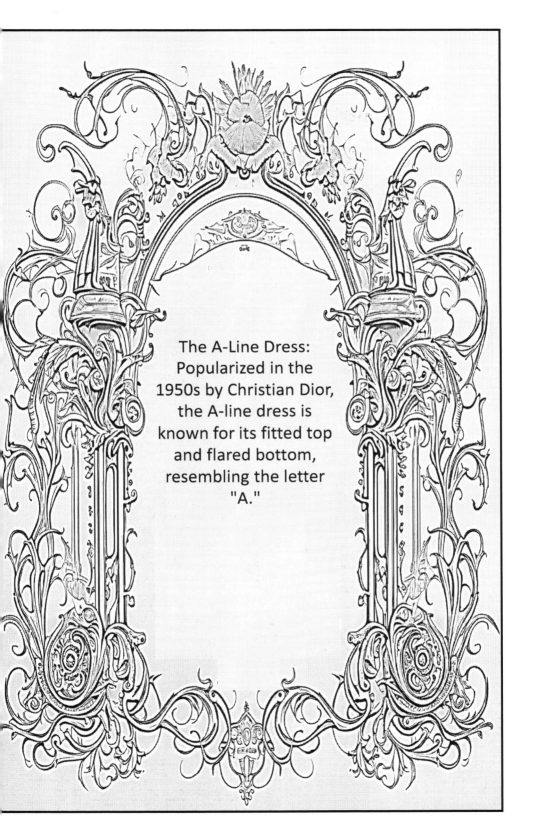

The A-Line Dress: Popularized in the 1950s by Christian Dior, the A-line dress is known for its fitted top and flared bottom, resembling the letter "A."

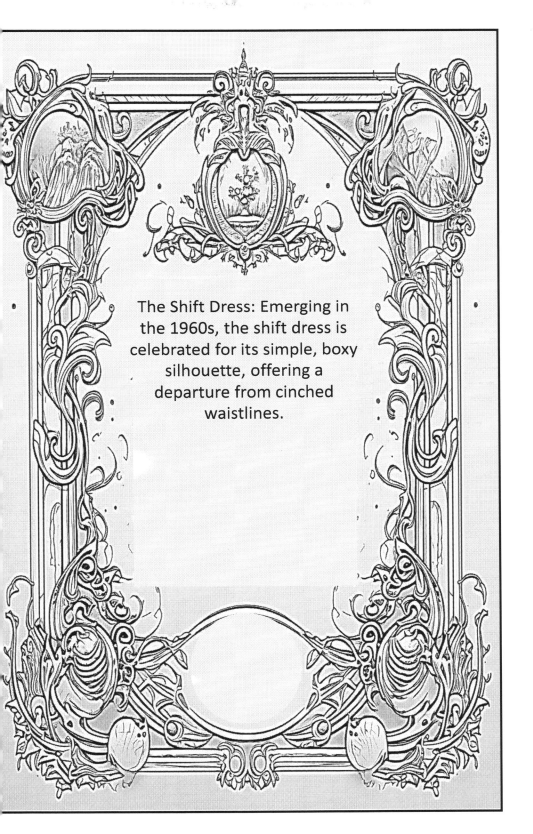

The Shift Dress: Emerging in the 1960s, the shift dress is celebrated for its simple, boxy silhouette, offering a departure from cinched waistlines.

Fashion Photography: The role of fashion photography in popularizing dresses and trends cannot be understated, with photographers like Richard Avedon and Mario Testino shaping the public's perception of fashion.

The Renaissance of
Vintage: The popularity
of vintage and retro
dresses reflects a
nostalgia for past fashion
eras and a commitment
to sustainable clothing
practices.

Award Show Red Carpets: Red carpet events like the Oscars have become pivotal moments for designers to showcase their most extravagant dresses, influencing fashion trends worldwide.

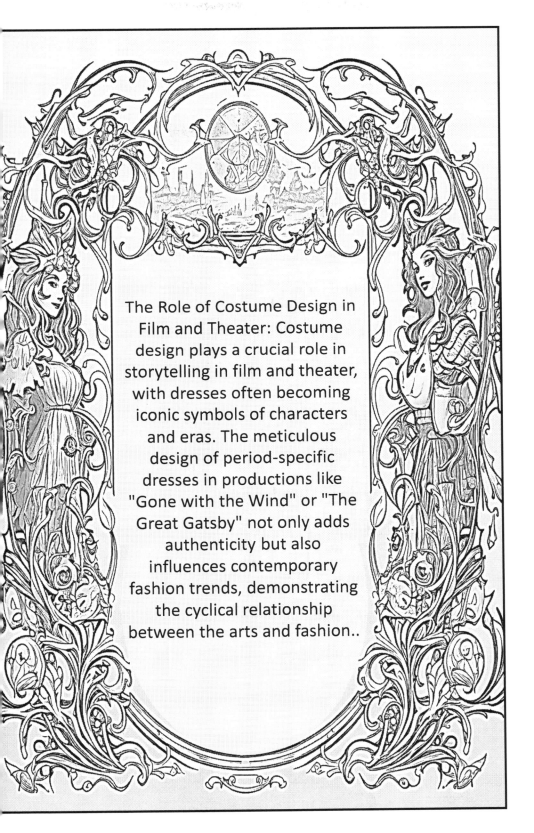

The Role of Costume Design in Film and Theater: Costume design plays a crucial role in storytelling in film and theater, with dresses often becoming iconic symbols of characters and eras. The meticulous design of period-specific dresses in productions like "Gone with the Wind" or "The Great Gatsby" not only adds authenticity but also influences contemporary fashion trends, demonstrating the cyclical relationship between the arts and fashion..

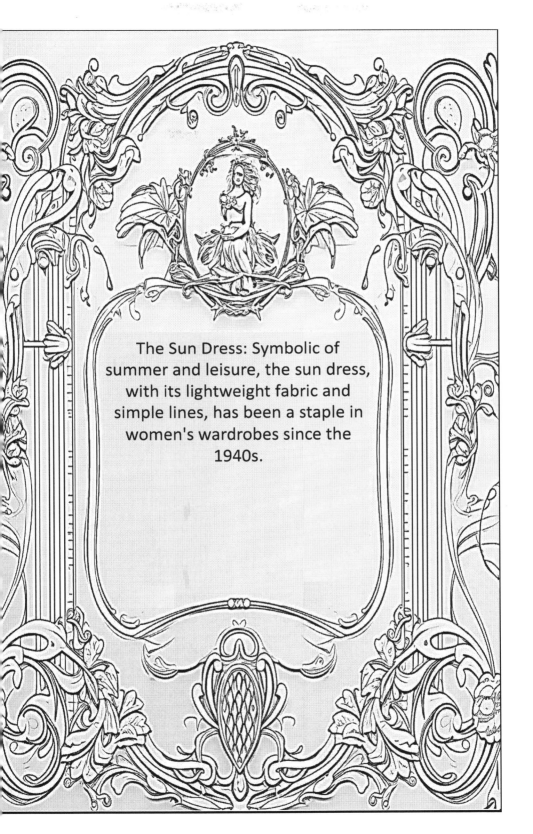

The Sun Dress: Symbolic of summer and leisure, the sun dress, with its lightweight fabric and simple lines, has been a staple in women's wardrobes since the 1940s.

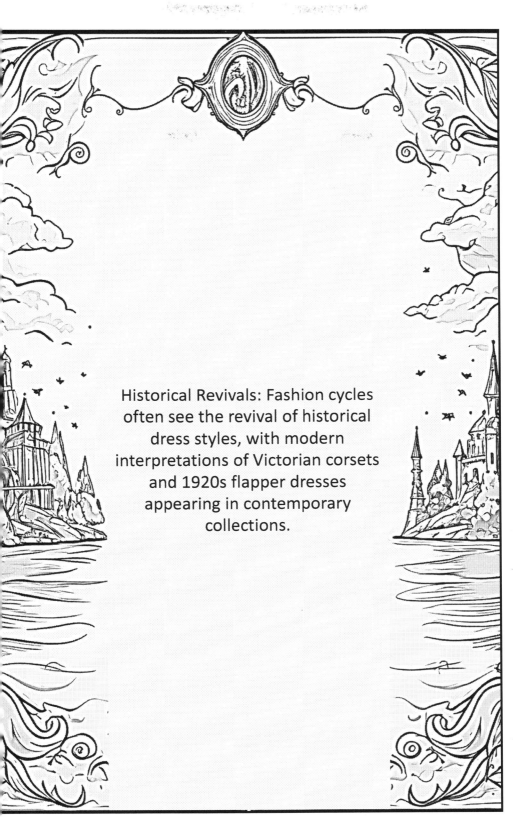

Historical Revivals: Fashion cycles often see the revival of historical dress styles, with modern interpretations of Victorian corsets and 1920s flapper dresses appearing in contemporary collections.

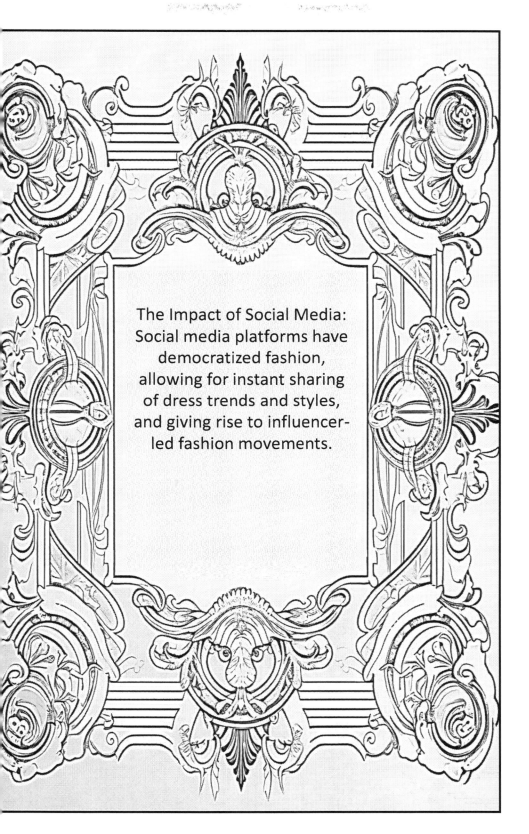

The Impact of Social Media: Social media platforms have democratized fashion, allowing for instant sharing of dress trends and styles, and giving rise to influencer-led fashion movements.

Sustainable Fabric Innovations: The development of eco-friendly fabrics, such as bamboo, organic cotton, and recycled polyester, is shaping the future of sustainable dressmaking.

Celebrity Wedding Dresses:
Wedding dresses worn by
celebrities often become
trendsetters, influencing bridal
fashion for years to come.

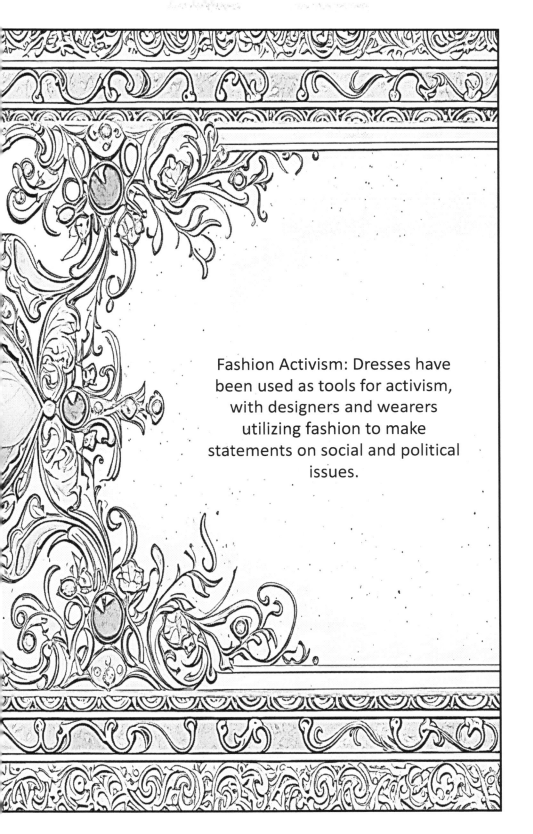

Fashion Activism: Dresses have been used as tools for activism, with designers and wearers utilizing fashion to make statements on social and political issues.

The Evolution of Wedding Dresses: From the multi-layered, heavily embellished gowns of the 19th century to today's diverse range of styles, wedding dresses have undergone significant evolution.

Digital Fashion: The rise of digital fashion and virtual dresses, wearable in digital environments, is expanding the definition of dress design and fashion.

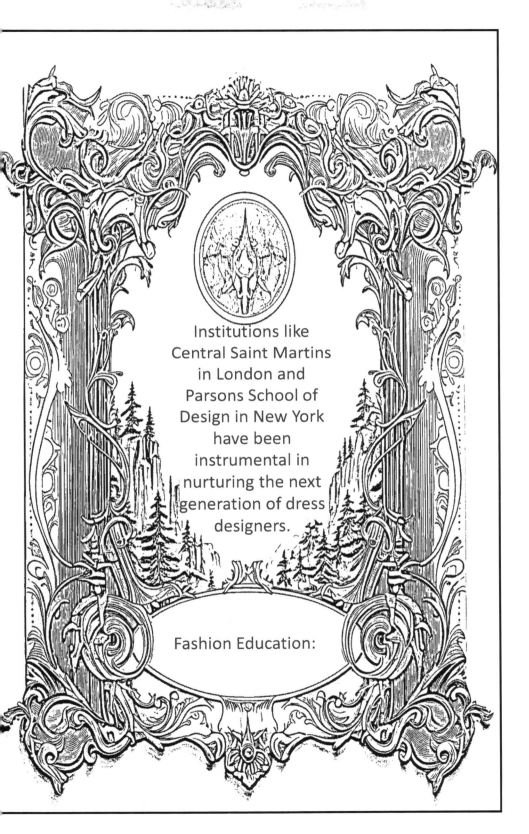

Institutions like Central Saint Martins in London and Parsons School of Design in New York have been instrumental in nurturing the next generation of dress designers.

Fashion Education:

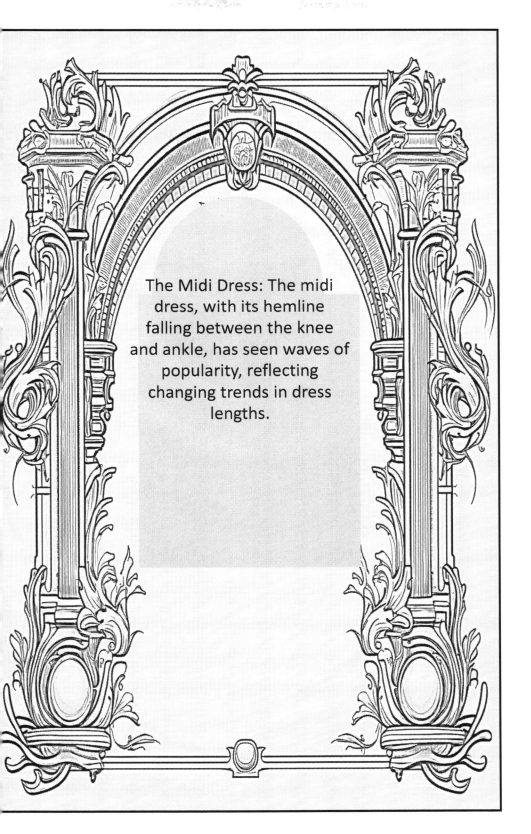

The Midi Dress: The midi dress, with its hemline falling between the knee and ankle, has seen waves of popularity, reflecting changing trends in dress lengths.

Ethnic and Cultural Dress Influences: Globalization has facilitated the cross-cultural exchange of dress styles, enriching the global fashion landscape.

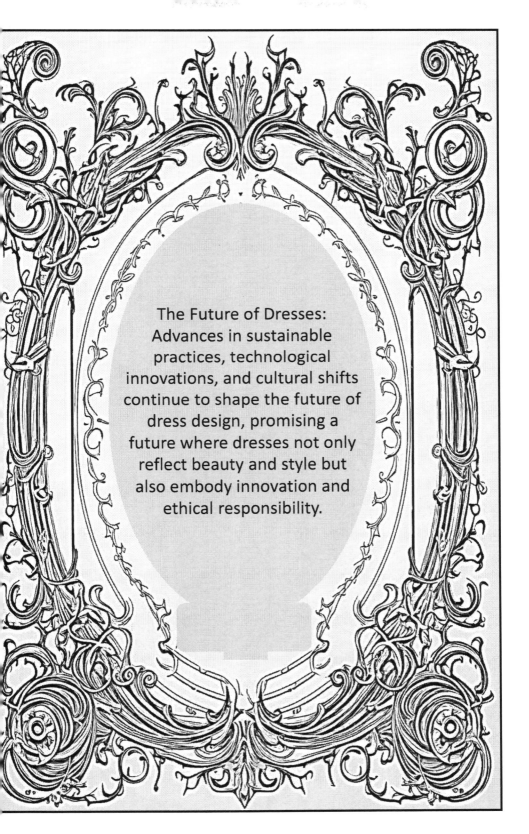

The Future of Dresses: Advances in sustainable practices, technological innovations, and cultural shifts continue to shape the future of dress design, promising a future where dresses not only reflect beauty and style but also embody innovation and ethical responsibility.

Made in the USA
Middletown, DE
23 August 2024

59051114R20057